WHY DO WE HAVE TO DO CHORES?

ROSE PEMBERTON

THE COMMON GOOD

PowerKiDS press.

New York

Published in 2019 by The Rosen Publishing Group, Inc.
29 East 21st Street, New York, NY 10010

First Edition

Editor: Jennifer Lombardo
Book Design: Tanya Dellaccio

Photo Credits: Cover Sergey Novikov/Shutterstock.com; p. 5 Africa Studio/Shutterstock.com; p. 7 Iakov Filimonov/Shutterstock.com; p. 9 LightField Studios/Shutterstock.com; p. 11 KidStock/Blend Images/Getty Images; p. 13 Steve Lyne/Dorling Kindersley/Getty Images; p. 15 Comstock/Stockbyte/Getty Images; p. 17 PR Image Factory/Shutterstock.com; p. 19 bbernard/Shutterstock.com; p. 21 Zurijeta/Shutterstock.com; p. 22 4 PM production/Shutterstock.com.

Cataloging-in-Publication Data

Names: Pemberton, Rose.
Title: Why do we have to do chores? / Rose Pemberton.
Description: New York : PowerKids Press, 2019. | Series: The common good | Includes index.
Identifiers: LCCN ISBN 9781538330845 (pbk.) | ISBN 9781538330838 (library bound) | ISBN 9781538330852 (6 pack)
Subjects: LCSH: Helping behavior–Juvenile literature. | Chores–Juvenile literature. | Housekeeping–Juvenile literature.
Classification: LCC HM1106.P46 2019 | DDC 302'.14–dc23

Manufactured in the United States of America

CPSIA Compliance Information: Batch #CS18PK: For Further Information contact Rosen Publishing, New York, New York at 1-800-237-9932

CONTENTS

A Family Community

Families come in many types and sizes, but every family is a community. A community is a group of people who live or work in the same place and care about the same things. Schools and neighborhoods are also communities. For most children, their family is the first and most important community they belong to.

When people do things that **benefit** everyone in their community, they're working toward the common good. Most people want what's best for their family members, so they often do things that are good for them. You can contribute, or give, to the common good of your family by doing chores.

7

Helping Your Family

Families are often very busy. Parents often have jobs and children have to go to school. They may also have homework and after-school **activities**. If everyone in the family does a few chores when they have time, nobody has to add too much more work to their day. When you do chores, you're helping to keep your family happy and running smoothly.

Doing chores teaches you to be **responsible** and shows your family members that you care about them. It also shows that you care about your home and your **belongings** by keeping them in good shape. By doing chores, you'll learn important life skills, such as how to wash clothes. If you have younger **siblings**, you'll also be setting a good example for them.

All Sorts of Chores

The types of chores you do are based on your age and the needs of your family. You might have to put dirty dishes in the dishwasher, or you might have to wash dishes in the sink. Younger children will often have simpler chores, such as feeding a pet, but they're still contributing to the good of the family.

Many children have chores they do every day. You might have to make your bed or pick up your toys. Other chores, such as taking out the trash, are done less often. Some chores need to be done as soon as your parent asks, but others just need to be done when you have free time. Whenever they're done, chores help keep your home clean and your family happy.

Working Together

Families are communities, and you can think of them sort of like teams. Family members use teamwork all the time. Chores teach you how to work with other people. You'll also learn to plan how to use your time. If you have basketball practice, homework, and chores, which do you do first?

By working as a team, your family can get all its chores done faster. This will give you more time to do other things as a family. You might watch a movie together or go to the park. It's always good when family members have more time to spend together.

Good for Everyone

You might not always want to do chores, but remember that they're a big help to your family members. You'll feel good knowing you're contributing to the common good of your family. The next time you're bored, pick an easy chore to do. Your family will **appreciate** it.

It's important for people to do chores even though the jobs might not be fun. No one wants to live in a dirty house or wear dirty clothes. Doing chores not only keeps your house and belongings looking nice, it teaches responsibility and respect, and it lets your family know you care. Everyone in your family benefits from doing chores.

GLOSSARY

activity: Something that someone does.

appreciate: To be thankful for something or someone.

belongings: The things a person owns.

benefit: To be helpful or useful to.

responsible: Able to be trusted to do what is right or to do the things that are expected or required.

sibling: A brother or a sister.

INDEX

WEBSITES

Due to the changing nature of Internet links, PowerKids Press has developed an online list of websites related to the subject of this book. This site is updated regularly. Please use this link to access the list: www.powerkidslinks.com/comg/chores